Pit Stop Secrets

By K. C. Kelley

The Child's World®

www.childsworld.com

The Child's World
www.childsworld.com

Published in the United States of America by
The Child's World®
1980 Lookout Drive • Mankato, MN 56003-1705
800-599-READ • www.childsworld.com

ACKNOWLEDGMENTS

The Child's World®:
Mary Berendes, Publishing Director

Produced by Shoreline Publishing Group LLC
President / Editorial Director: James Buckley, Jr.
Designer: Tom Carling, carlingdesign.com
Assistant Editor: Jim Gigliotti

Photo Credits:
Cover: Joe Robbins.
Interior: All photos by Joe Robbins.

**LIBRARY OF CONGRESS
CATALOGING-IN-PUBLICATION DATA**

Kelley, K. C.
   Pit stop secrets / by K.C. Kelley.
      p. cm. — (The world of NASCAR)
   Includes bibliographical references and index.
   ISBN 978-1-60253-080-5 (library bound : alk.
paper)
   1. Pit crews—United States—Juvenile literature.
2. Stock car racing—United States—Juvenile
literature. 3. NASCAR (Association)—Juvenile
literature. I. Title. II. Series.
   GV1029.9.S74K453 2008
   796.72—dc22
                                    2007049080

Contents

[OPPOSITE]
*Things are crazy on pit road during a race!
How do these highly trained experts do
their job? Let's take a look!*

Standing Still but Going Fast

FOR THREE OR FOUR HOURS DURING A NASCAR
race, cars zoom around the tracks at top speed. Their
drivers have the pedal to the metal—getting as much
speed out of their cars as they can. The whole point of
the race, after all, is to win. And you win by being fastest.

However, some of the most important parts of every
NASCAR race come when the car is standing still!

You can count all seven members of the "over-the-wall" pit crew as they race to service Ryan Newman's car.

Every little thing helps save speed. This pit crew member is using a blowtorch to melt off bits of rubber that have stuck to the smooth surface of the racing tire.

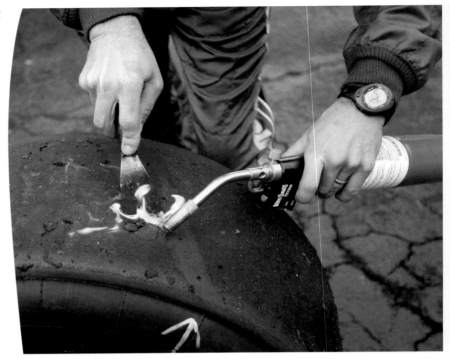

A driver might have the fastest car on the track when it's moving, but if his pit crew isn't just as fast, that driver will find himself at the back of the pack. Pit crews are highly trained people who give the driver and his car everything they need to succeed.

Just like your family car, NASCAR stock cars need fuel. They need new tires. But your parents might send your car to the shop for a day or two, or they might take 10 minutes to fill the car with gas. A NASCAR pit crew has just seconds to do all that work. Every second a driver spends in the pits is a second he is not on the track racing at top speed. Just because a driver has to stop for gas or new tires doesn't mean the race stops.

While a driver's crew works feverishly, his opponents roar around the track, gaining precious time. (Of course, his opponents will have to stop later on, too, to get their own gas.)

The pit crew members have to do a series of very difficult jobs and they can't make a single mistake. The difference in a NASCAR race between Victory Lane and second place can be fractions of a second. A pit crew that can gain its driver those fractions might be able to celebrate a victory.

In stock car racing's early days, pit crews were often just friends of the drivers who knew something about cars. They were not professionals, and they usually didn't practice. They just showed up on race day to have fun and help their pals. Today's crews, however, are full-time professionals. All the crews train long and hard to become perfect—and fast!

In a pit stop today, the seven members of the pit crew might change four tires, fill the car with gas, get the driver some water, and clean a windscreen. And they can do it all in less time than it took you to read the last page. They can do all that work in less than 20 seconds! Sometimes it can be even less than 15 seconds!

Read on to meet these hard-working pit crew members and find out how they do their jobs.

Many of today's NASCAR pit crews lift weights, run, and work out with a trainer. The hard work between races pays off when they can do their jobs a few seconds faster.

2

Teaming Up for Speed

FOR A NASCAR TEAM, REACHING VICTORY LANE
means many hours of hard work. For pit crews, it means
practice, practice, practice. Most teams practice for hours
and hours during the week to get ready for weekend
racing. Their goal is to finish a typical pit stop as fast as
possible and get the job done safely.

Being on a pit crew is nearly a full-time job. All the
pit crew members work for the racing team, just as
the driver does. Their work on the pit is their main job.
However, they might also help build engines or work on
another one of the car's systems. Most NASCAR teams
have a person who is the pit crew trainer. He schedules
the crew members' workouts and makes sure they're
ready to roll on race days.

These pit crew members have worked their way
to the top, just as athletes in other sports. They worked

[OPPOSITE]
*It's a rainbow of
racing colors as the
teams line up in pit
road for the National
Anthem before a race.*

9

Pit Power!

NASCAR drivers win on the track. Their crews win in the pits. But while drivers get dozens of chances for victory, there's only one World Pit Crew Championship. At this event, crews are timed on how fast they can change four tires, fill their race car with 40 gallons (151 l) of gas, and then push the car 40 yards (37 m). They need strength, speed, accuracy, and perfect timing.

In 2007, the crew of Ryan Newman's No. 12 car won the title for the third year in a row. Two members of another crew set a new record by changing two rear tires in less than 14 seconds!

The Pit Crew Championship is a great event for the crew to win . . . but they'd all still rather win races!

at smaller races to build their skills and knowledge. Pit crews are so important that there are even schools where workers can learn even more about these key jobs.

"Teamwork is everything in our sport," said Sammy Johns, the vice president of Evernham Motorsports. He used to be the **crew chief** for driver Jeremy Mayfield. Now he works with the crew chiefs of all of his team's cars. The crew chiefs lead the teams on and off the track. A crew chief guides a team's training and **strategy**. During the race, he sits on a small platform above the team. He is in touch with the driver and the crew via radio headsets. He also gets information from **spotters** above the track and **sensors** in the car.

Crew chiefs today also use computers to keep track of how much fuel the car is using and how other cars in the race are doing. The computer tells the chief how many laps have been run and gives him the tools he needs to "call the race."

One of the crew chief's biggest jobs is deciding when it's time "to pit." Using all of his experience and all the information he has gathered, he has to tell the driver when to come to the pits. His decision can mean the difference between winning and losing a race. Pit

The crew chief and his helpers sit above pit road on platforms. They study computers and video monitors throughout the race.

too early, and you might lose time. Pit too late, and you might not have time to catch up. Skip a pit, and you might run out of gas before the race ends! It's a careful balancing act.

Looks like driver Travis Kvapil (right) isn't sure he likes what crew chief Mike Beam is telling him.

When the yellow caution flag comes out and drivers slow down, pit crews often spring into action.

Different flag colors mean different things. Green flags signal the start of a race. Yellow flags mean caution. Races stop when red flags appear. And, of course, the checkered flag means the winner has crossed the finish line.

"You can do all the planning you want," Johns said, "but it all seems to go out the window by the time the **green flag** drops [to start the race]."

The chief has to make the decision about 15 to 20 laps before it's time to pit. Drivers also often come in to the pits during yellow-flag caution periods. These periods happen when there is an accident. The drivers must slow down to the same speed while the track is cleared. There is no passing during a yellow-flag period.

Once the decision to come in to the pits is made, it's up to the pit crew. As that driver comes to a halt in his pit stall, the crew members go "over the wall."

Time to go to work!

3

Swappin' Rubber

AS THE DRIVER SQUEALS TO A HALT FOR HIS PIT

stop, the crew goes over the wall. The first man to the car is the jack man. "He's the key," Sammy Johns said. The jack man uses a six- to seven-pound (3-kg) aluminum jack. This tool lifts one side of the car completely off the ground. NASCAR jacks use **air pressure** so that the jack man needs only one pump to lift the car. Most jack men are big and strong—many are former college football players. The jack man can't make a mistake; if he doesn't do his job just right, the crew can't even start its work.

Once the jack man has raised the car, the tire changers get to work. Most teams change tires three to five times during a race. The speed, pounding action, and high heat of the race make tires unsafe after 100 to 150 miles (161 to 241 km), depending on the track. NASCAR supplies all the tires to each team. However, each team chooses how much air pressure to put in the tires. Tires are so important to a race car that five of the seven pit crew members are involved with changing them.

Along with one jack man, each crew also has two tire carriers and two tire changers (one pair for each of the front and rear wheels). The front- and rear-tire changers replace the tires. They start on the right side,

[OPPOSITE]
The front and rear tire changers are on their knees. The blue hose sends air to the special wrench used to remove the tires.

15

farthest away from the pit wall. Using a special **air gun** on a rubber hose, each changer loosens five **lug nuts** on each tire. The nuts attach the wheels to the car. The air guns loosen the five nuts in less than a second. Zing, zing, zing, zing, zing . . . almost as fast as you can read that, the lug nuts are loose and the tire is off.

Front- and rear-tire carriers work with the two tire changers. Tire carriers are the strong men of the pit crew. They heave 80- to 90-pound (36- to 41-kg) tires around like you'd flip a donut. The carriers jump over the wall carrying tires for the right side. They hold the old tires and then hang the new tires in place for the tire changers. Then these mini-teams of carrier and changer race around to do the same thing on the left side of the car.

"It can be like a ballet," said Johns. "You've got these big tires, running men, and the flying hose of the air gun."

It can be dangerous, too. With all those heavy tires, the speeding cars, and the crowded pit road, accidents do happen. Since 2005, all pit crew members have worn helmets much like those worn by the driver. Pit crew members have been hit by cars, dropped tires on their feet, or pinched their fingers. However, they all work very hard to make safety as important as speed.

Pit stops might look like a ballet, but it's one crazy dance!

Pit crew members do more than just fill gas and change tires. The crew members who don't go "over the wall" reach out with poles to clean windows or to hand the driver a water bottle.

Inside NASCAR Tires

One company gives all NASCAR teams the same tires. But each car and driver likes their tires inflated a certain way. After practice laps, the teams inspect the tires. They measure them in several ways to see how they're wearing down. This will give them clues on how to make their car move even faster.

First, they check three "wear holes." A device is put in the holes to see how deep they are compared to how deep they were before the practice laps. Sometimes there is so much loose rubber, the teams have to use a blowtorch to remove it so they can make their depth measurements.

The teams also measure the temperature of the tires. If the temperature is higher in the middle than on the edges, that means they put too much air in. A higher temperature at the edges might mean a car isn't balanced in the best way possible.

Turns out "reading" tires can help a crew make a race car go faster.

4

Gas and Go!

CHANGING TIRES IS A BIG PART OF A PIT STOP.
But without this next part, those tires won't be able to
move. Just like your family car, NASCAR racers need
gasoline to make their engines go—and their tires turn.
The crew has to make sure the car has enough gas to
finish the race—or at least make it to the next pit stop.
Too many drivers have seen victory disappear as their
fuel tank runs dry before the end.

Knowing when to put in fuel and how much to use
are key decisions of the crew chief. Computer sensors
help them plan how much more they'll need before the
next pit stop. The driver also has a fuel pressure gauge,
but Johns said drivers rarely use it. That's really the job
of the crew.

"To make sure we're putting in enough fuel, we use
a computer program," Johns said. "We count laps and
weigh the fuel before and after the pit stop. That tells
how much we got in there. Then we work out miles per
gallon and laps per gallon."

[OPPOSITE]
*Before the gas goes
in the car, a crew
member has to fill the
large gas cans.*

19

Once they know how much fuel they need, it's time for a pit stop and more hard work by the pit crew.

Two members of the pit crew—the gas man and the **catch-can** man—are responsible for fueling the car. All NASCAR team use a special blend of gasoline provided by the same company. The gas man carries an 11-gallon (42 l) gas tank over the wall. He puts the can's nozzle into a special fuel port at the back left side of the car.

Meanwhile, his partner, the catch-can man, puts a special tool into a vent at the rear of the car. This lets the gas flow fast and free into the car. No hoses or dials or

Body Work

A basic pit stop fuels the car and changes tires. But lots of other things can go wrong during a race, and pit stops are a team's only chance to make repairs. Because crews have so little time, they can usually only fix broken or missing parts of the car's body. How the air flows over a car is very important, so even a small dent or missing part can slow down a car.

In the pits, teams can replace a hood, fender, nose, or rear **spoilers** or wings. You might see a crew member use a hammer to pound out a dent. If a car is more seriously damaged, it can be taken to the garage for repairs, such as to replace a transmission or fix a brake. A team can't win if that happens, but if they can get the car back on the track, they can earn a few extra points depending on what place they finish. Teams want to win the race first, but if they can't, they try to earn points to help them toward a season-long championship.

credit cards needed! The catch-can man also collects any fuel that spills over, keeping it off the track. He then holds the first can, while a second can is poured into the car. And they usually do all that in fewer than 10 seconds.

Safety is even more important for these two members than others. As with anyone who works around dangerous stuff, they take extra precautions.

"Fire is the worst thing we can have happen in the pits," said Johns. To prevent fires, the fuel is carefully handled and collected. The gas man wears a fire-resistant apron and a special helmet that has fans that blow in air and keep out fumes. Like all the other crew members, the gas men wear fire suits. These full-body jumpsuits are made of special fabric that is resistant to fire.

If gas is the stuff that makes the cars go, these are the guys who make the gas go!

The black apron on the gas man (left) protects him from any fuel that might spill while he fills the tank.

5

Time to Pit!

LET'S TAKE A TRIP THROUGH AN ENTIRE PIT STOP

and see how speed and teamwork help win NASCAR races.

With about 250 of the race's 400 laps remaining, a race team thinks it might be time to pit. They've been on the same tires for 150 miles (241 km), and the computer says they're running low on gas. The crew chief

To follow the action of this pit stop by driver Ryan Newman's crew, just follow the numbers from one to eight.

Drivers look for a sign with their team number (Jimmie Johnson's No. 48 is shown here) to find their pit stall.

speaks with the driver on the radio. They talk about what the driver should do.

"Bring it in next time around," he says. "We'll do four and fuel." He means four new tires and a full load of gasoline.

"Kinda thirsty here, make sure I get some water," the driver says in return. "Also, I'm a little **loose** on the left front. Can you fix it?"

"Sure, you got it…see you in a minute."

The driver then finishes turn 3 and starts gearing down as he heads for the entrance to pit row. At most tracks, that entry is before turn 4. As soon as he hits pit road, he has to slow down. Unlike the rest of the race track, pit road has a speed limit. This is for the safety of the crews and the drivers. The speed is different for each track, depending on race day conditions. A driver might have to go from 160 miles (257 km) per hour to 35 or 40 (56 or 64 km) very quickly.

As the driver rolls down pit road, he watches for his car's number sign. A crew member reaches out this sign on a long pole. The driver tries to stop his car right at that sign. Each car is assigned a space on pit road. Any car that goes even a little bit into a neighboring space can be **penalized** by officials.

The second the car stops rolling, the seven pit crew members are over the wall!

The jack man leads the way, lugging his jack. He runs around the back end of the car, slides the jack underneath, and—bingo!—the right side of the car is up. At the same time, the front and rear tire changers are loosening lug nuts on the right-side tires. The tire carriers exchange new tires for old and then help keep the air-gun hoses from tangling. Within seconds, the right-side tires are changed, and the jack man and the tire crews sprint to the left side of the car.

Meanwhile, a crew member reaches out from behind the wall with a "driver-service" pole. This holds a drink bottle that the driver reaches out and takes. He'll drink it down with a straw through his helmet visor. While the driver drinks, so does the car. Behind him, the gas man has already poured in the first can of gas and is

On most NASCAR racers, a small triangle sticker points to the spot on the car where the jack man should place his jack. This spot will let him do the best and fastest tire-raising move.

Keep It Fair!

While a team's pit-crew members dress in a rainbow of colors, other people in the pit are dressed in white jumpuits. These are NASCAR officials, who watch each pit stop carefully. NASCAR wants to make sure that all the people involved in the race are safe—and that they follow all the rules. To make sure the race is fair, these officials make sure that only seven crew members go over the wall, for example. They make sure the lug nuts are safe, to keep a tire from falling off and causing an accident. They keep track of all the old tires to make sure the pit road is safe.

A team that breaks a rule might be called back to the pits, costing valuable time. Teams can also be penalized laps, time, or points.

lifting the second one into place. The gas man and catch-can man can empty both cans in less than 15 seconds.

Back to the jack man: He has reached the left side and jacked up the car again. But he has another job. Remember that the driver said he was "loose"? That means he was having a little trouble keeping the car on a straight line in turns. To fix this, the jack man makes a small adjustment to the way the car is balanced. As the tire changers work, he takes out a small wrench. He puts this in a hole on the outside of the car and makes a quick turn. The team hopes this small adjustment will help the driver gain a tiny bit of extra speed.

Then the jack man watches the tire changers and the team. He also watches the traffic behind his driver in the busy pit road. His crew chief is also on the radio giving him updates. His left hand is raised up.

Now the way is clear. The instant he sees the gas can pulled away and the final lug nuts tightened, he drops the jack and his arm. This is a signal to the driver to hit the gas!

The driver roars out into pit road, quickly hitting that speed limit. As soon as he reaches the end of that road, he'll be at top speed in just seconds.

Go, go, go! As the final drops of fuel go in (rear) and the jack comes out (far right), the crew signals the driver to get going!

High fives all around! After a hard day at the track, the crew members know their skills might have given their team the edge to win!

Speaking of just seconds . . . all the action in this entire chapter took fewer than 20 seconds!

The crew members exchange some high-fives and pick up their gear. They'll have a few moments to catch their breath before they spring into action again. After the race, of course, they hope they can celebrate in Victory Lane. Every NASCAR driver knows that's a place he can't visit without a lot of help from his hard-working pit crew.

Pit Stop Step-by-Step

1 Driver pulls into pit stall, stopping exactly in front of a sign with his car number.

2 As car comes to a stop, seven members of the pit crew hop over the wall and swarm around the car.

3 The jack man quickly raises the right side of the car, farthest from the pit wall.

4 While the car is being jacked up, the gas man starts pouring in the first of two cans of gas into the car's tank.

5 As soon as the right side is off the ground, the two tire changers use their air guns to loosen five lug nuts. They pull off the used tires and hand them to . . .

6 . . . the two tire carriers, who swap out the old tires for new ones that they have carried over the wall.

7 While the tire carriers are removing the old tires and getting two more new ones, the tire changers finish tightening the tires on the right side.

8 The jack man lowers the right side and then rushes to the left side and raises it off the ground.

9 The tire changers and tire carriers repeat their work, loosening and removing old tires and "hanging" two new ones.

10 As the final tire is tightened, the gas man finishes putting in his second can. The jack man lowers the car and the driver roars the engine to get the car back into the race. Total time spent to complete all these tasks: about 15 seconds.

Glossary

air gun   a hand tool that uses air pressure to loosen or tighten lug nuts

air pressure   the force with which air within an object presses against that object

catch-can   a small tool used by the pit crew to grab fuel before it can spill

crew chief   the person in charge of the members of a NASCAR race team

green flag   the signal for the start of a race

loose   a racing term meaning that the rear of a car is drifting toward the wall while turning

lug nuts   small hexagons of metal that hold onto bolts

penalized   given some form of punishment

sensors   parts of a machine or computer that take in information from the outside and report it to the user

spoilers   strips of metal at the front or back of a car that help air flow smoothly over the surface

spotters   crew members who sit high above the racetrack and report conditions to the driver and crew

strategy   the plan of attack for a race

Find Out More

BOOKS

Eyewitness NASCAR
By James Buckley Jr.
DK Publishing, 2005
This photo-filled book takes you inside the world of NASCAR. See close-up pictures of engines and other gear, meet the heroes of the sport, and see more photos of pit-stop and racing action.

NASCAR in the Pits
By Mike Kennedy and Mark Stewart
Lerner Publications, 2007
Here's another "inside" look at how NASCAR pit crews train for the weekend races, do their jobs in split seconds, and mean the difference between winning and losing.

NASCAR Record & Fact Book
Sporting News Books, 2008
Loaded with facts and figures about current drivers and NASCAR history, this handy reference source also includes a stock car racing glossary and pit stop details.

Pit Pass
By Bob Woods
Readers' Digest Children's Publishing, 2005
Take an "inside" look at NASCAR tracks, drivers, cars, and gear.

WEB SITES

Visit our Web site for lots of links about NASCAR:
www.childsworld.com/links

Note to Parents, Teachers, and Librarians: We routinely check our Web links to make sure they're safe, active sites—so encourage your readers to check them out!

Index

ABOUT THE AUTHOR

K. C. Kelley is a writer who lives in Santa Barbara, California. He has written many books on sports for young readers. He wishes that his local gas station was as fast as a NASCAR pit crew!